— THE STRESS-LESS —
HANDBOOK

Practical Strategies for Overcoming Anxiety and Thriving in the Modern World.

UMAR PLUMMER

DEDICATION

To my family and friends, who have supported and encouraged me throughout my journey towards a stress-less life.

To the mental health professionals who have taught me valuable coping strategies and helped me navigate challenges.

To anyone who is struggling with stress and anxiety, I hope this book can serve as a helpful resource on your own journey towards a healthy, fulfilling life.

TABLE OF **CONTENTS**

AUTHOR'S NOTE

Writing this book has been a labor of love and a personal journey for me. As someone who has struggled with anxiety and stress in the past, I know firsthand how challenging it can be to manage these emotions and live a healthy, fulfilling life.

I hope that the strategies and techniques outlined in this book will be helpful to others who are struggling with stress and anxiety. Remember, managing these emotions is a lifelong process, and it's important to be kind to yourself and seek support when needed.

Thank you for reading and I hope this book serves as a helpful guide on your journey towards well-being.

INTRODUCTION

Anxiety and stress are a normal part of life, but when they become overwhelming and interfere with our daily functioning, it's time to take action. The Stress-Less Handbook is here to help you find practical strategies for managing anxiety and stress in the modern world.

We'll start by exploring what anxiety and stress are, the causes and effects of these emotions, and how they can impact our physical and mental health. Then, we'll delve into specific strategies for managing stress, including exercise and physical activity, mindfulness and meditation, good sleep hygiene, and more.

In addition to these self-help strategies, we'll also discuss when it might be necessary to seek professional help from a mental health professional, and how to choose the right therapist or counselor for your needs.
But managing stress isn't just about tackling problems head-on; it's also about taking care of yourself. In this book, we'll explore the importance of self-care and provide practical tips for incorporating self-care into your daily routine.

Finally, we'll look at how to build resilience, find balance, set boundaries, and seek support from loved ones as you journey towards a stress-less life. Remember, managing anxiety and stress is a lifelong process, but with the right tools and mindset, you can learn to thrive in the modern world.

Chapter 01

UNDERSTANDING ANXIETY AND STRESS

Anxiety and stress are a normal part of life, but when they become overwhelming and interfere with our daily functioning, it's time to take action. In this chapter, we'll explore what anxiety and stress are, the causes of these emotions, and the effects they can have on our physical and mental health.

Defining Anxiety and Stress
Anxiety and stress are two closely related emotions that we all experience from time to time. Anxiety is a feeling of unease, such as worry or fear, that can be mild or severe. Stress is a response to a challenge or demand. It can be caused by both positive and negative experiences, and it can have physical and emotional effects on the body.

The Causes of Anxiety and Stress
There are many potential causes of anxiety and stress. Some common causes include:
- Work-related stress: Deadlines, demanding bosses, and workload can all contribute to stress.
- Personal relationships: Conflict with friends or loved ones, or the demands of caring for others, can cause stress.
- Financial stress: Worrying about money, paying bills, and managing debt can be a major source of stress.
- Health concerns: Illness, injury, or the fear of getting sick can all contribute to anxiety and stress.
- Life changes: Moving, starting a new job, getting married, or having a baby can be exciting, but they can also be stressful.

Chapter 01

The Effects of Anxiety and Stress on the Body and Mind

Anxiety and stress can have both physical and emotional effects on the body. Physical symptoms of anxiety and stress can include:
- Headaches
- Muscle tension or pain
- Chest pain
- Fatigue
- Change in appetite
- Difficulty sleeping

Emotional symptoms of anxiety and stress can include:
- Feelings of worry or fear
- Difficulty concentrating
- Irritability
- Restlessness

If left unchecked, anxiety and stress can lead to more serious health problems, such as high blood pressure, heart disease, and depression. That's why it's important to learn how to manage anxiety and stress, and to seek help when necessary.

In the next chapter, we'll explore how to identify the things that cause you stress, and how to understand the impact they have on your life.

IDENTIFYING YOUR STRESS TRIGGERS

In order to effectively manage stress, it's important to first identify what is causing it. In this chapter, we'll explore how to identify the things that cause you to stress, and how to understand the impact they have on your life.

Identifying the Things That Cause You Stress

There are many potential causes of stress, and what triggers stress for one person may not affect another person in the same way. Some common stress triggers include:
- Work-related issues, such as deadlines, demanding bosses, or a heavy workload
- Personal relationships, including conflicts with friends or loved ones, or the demands of caring for others
- Financial concerns, such as worries about money, paying bills, or managing debt
- Health issues, including illness, injury, or the fear of getting sick
- Life changes, like moving, starting a new job, getting married, or having a baby

To identify your own stress triggers, it can be helpful to keep a stress journal. In this journal, record the things that cause you to stress, as well as how you feel and behave when you're stressed. Over time, patterns may emerge, and you may start to see what situations or activities tend to trigger stress for you.

8

Chapter 02

Understanding How Your Stress Triggers Affect You

Once you've identified your stress triggers, it's important to understand how they affect you. Do certain situations or activities always cause you stress? Do you tend to feel and behave differently when you're stressed?

By understanding the impact of your stress triggers, you can start to develop coping strategies that work for you. For example, if you tend to get overwhelmed by work-related stress, you might try breaking larger tasks into smaller ones, setting aside dedicated time for focused work, or asking for help when you need it.

In the next chapter, we'll delve into specific strategies for managing stress, including exercise and physical activity, mindfulness and meditation, good sleep hygiene, and more.

PRACTICAL STRATEGIES FOR MANAGING STRESS

Now that you've identified your stress triggers and understand how they affect you, it's time to start developing strategies for managing stress. In this chapter, we'll explore several practical strategies that can help you cope with stress and improve your overall well-being.

Exercise and Physical Activity as Stress Management Tools

Exercise and physical activity can be powerful tools for managing stress. When you engage in physical activity, your body releases endorphins, which are chemicals that can help improve your mood and reduce feelings of stress. Exercise can also help you sleep better, boost your energy levels, and improve your overall physical health.

There are many ways to incorporate exercise and physical activity into your routine, regardless of your fitness level or interests. Some options might include:
- Going for a walk or jog
- Taking a yoga or Pilates class
- Joining a sports team or club
- Lifting weights or doing other strength training exercises
- Going for a swim
- Riding a bike

<h1 style="text-align:center">Chapter 03</h1>

The Benefits of Mindfulness and Meditation

Mindfulness is the practice of bringing your attention to the present moment, without judgment. It involves paying attention to your thoughts, feelings, and surroundings in a non-reactive way. Research has shown that mindfulness can help reduce stress, improve concentration, and enhance overall well-being.

There are many ways to incorporate mindfulness into your life, including:

- Practicing meditation: Meditation involves focusing your attention on a specific object, thought, or activity, and letting other thoughts come and go without reacting to them. There are many different types of meditation, so you can experiment to find what works best for you.
- Engaging in mindful breathing: Focusing on your breath can be a simple and effective way to bring your attention to the present moment. Try closing your eyes and paying attention to your breath as it moves in and out of your body.
- Engaging in mindful movement: Activities like yoga and tai chi can be a great way to combine mindfulness with physical activity.

The Power of Good Sleep Hygiene

Getting enough quality sleep is essential for managing stress and improving overall health. Good sleep hygiene refers to the habits and practices that can help you get a good night's sleep. Some tips for improving your sleep hygiene include:

- Establishing a regular bedtime routine
- Creating a sleep-friendly environment (e.g., keeping the bedroom cool, dark, and quiet)
- Avoiding caffeine and alcohol close to bedtime
- Limiting screen time before bed
- Exercising during the day

Nutrition and Stress Management

What you eat and drink can have a big impact on your stress levels. While it's important to nourish your body with a healthy, balanced diet, certain foods and drinks can have a calming effect on the body. Some options might include:

- Foods rich in complex carbohydrates, such as whole grains and legumes, which can help boost serotonin levels and improve mood
- Foods high in omega-3 fatty acids, such as fatty fish and nuts, which may have a calming effect on the body
- Herbal teas, such as chamomile or lavender, which may have a relaxing effect

It's also important to stay hydrated, as being dehydrated can contribute to feelings of stress and fatigue.

Chapter 03

Time Management and Organization

Feeling overwhelmed and stretched thin can be a major source of stress. To manage your time more effectively, try the following strategies:
- Make a to-do list: Writing down your tasks can help you feel more organized and in control.
- Set priorities: Identify the most important tasks and focus on them first.
- Break larger tasks into smaller ones: This can make tasks feel more manageable and help you make progress more quickly.
- Allow yourself breaks: Taking short breaks can help you recharge and come back to tasks with renewed energy.
- Delegate tasks when possible: If you have the support of others, don't be afraid to ask for help.

enough quality sleep is essential for managing stress and improving overall health. Good sleep hygiene refers to the habits and practices that can help you get a good night's sleep. Some tips for improving your sleep hygiene include:
- Establishing a regular bedtime routine
- Creating a sleep-friendly environment (e.g., keeping the bedroom cool, dark, and quiet)
- Avoiding caffeine and alcohol close to bedtime
- Limiting screen time before bed
- Exercising during the day

Chapter 03

Communication and Conflict Resolution

Effective communication is essential for managing stress in personal relationships. When you communicate openly and honestly with others, it can help prevent misunderstandings and resolve conflicts more quickly. Here are some tips for improving your communication skills:

- Use "I" statements: Instead of saying "you did this," try saying "I feel this way when you do this." This helps to express your own feelings and perspectives, rather than assigning blame.
- Listen actively: Pay attention to what the other person is saying, and try to understand their perspective.
- Be open to compromise: Try to find a solution that works for both parties.
- Seek help when necessary: If you're having trouble resolving a conflict, it might be helpful to seek the help of a mediator or counselor.

In the next chapter, we'll explore when it might be necessary to seek professional help from a mental health professional, and how to choose the right therapist or counselor for your needs.

SEEKING PROFESSIONAL HELP

Sometimes, managing stress and anxiety on your own is not enough. In these cases, seeking the help of a mental health professional can be an important step toward improving your well-being. In this chapter, we'll explore when to seek help from a mental health professional, and how to choose the right therapist or counselor for your needs.

When to Seek Help from a Mental Health Professional
There are several signs that it might be time to seek help from a mental health professional:
- Your stress and anxiety are interfering with your daily life, such as your work or relationships
- You're struggling to cope with a major life change, such as a divorce or the loss of a loved one
- You're having thoughts of self-harm or suicide
- You're experiencing persistent physical symptoms, such as headaches or stomach pain, that are not due to a medical condition
- You've tried self-help strategies, such as exercise and mindfulness, but they haven't been enough to improve your symptoms

If you're experiencing any of these symptoms, it's important to seek help from a mental health professional.

Chapter 04

Choosing the Right Therapist or Counselor

When choosing a mental health professional, it's important to find someone who is a good fit for you. Here are some things to consider:

- Expertise: Look for a therapist or counselor who has experience working with people who have similar concerns to yours.
- Credentials: Check to make sure the therapist or counselor is licensed in your state.
- Approach: There are many different therapeutic approaches, such as cognitive-behavioral therapy (CBT), dialectical behavior therapy (DBT), and others. Consider what approach might work best for you.
- Comfort level: It's important to feel comfortable with your therapist or counselor. Trust your instincts and choose someone you feel comfortable talking to.

The Benefits of Therapy and Counseling

Seeking the help of a mental health professional can provide many benefits. Some of the benefits of therapy and counseling include:

- A safe and confidential place to explore your thoughts and feelings
- Support and guidance as you work through challenges and make positive changes

Chapter 04

- A chance to learn new coping strategies and skills
- Improved communication and relationships with others
- Enhanced self-awareness and self-esteem

In the next chapter, we'll explore the importance of self-care and provide practical tips for incorporating self-care into your daily routine.

17

SELF-CARE AND STRESS MANAGEMENT

Self-care is an essential part of managing stress and maintaining overall well-being. It's about taking care of your physical, emotional, and mental needs in order to feel your best. In this chapter, we'll explore the importance of self-care and provide practical tips for incorporating self-care into your daily routine.

The Importance of Self-Care

Self-care is often the first thing to do when we're feeling overwhelmed or stressed, but it's more important than ever to make time for self-care during these times. Here are some reasons why self-care is so important:

- It helps you manage stress: When you practice self-care, you're taking care of yourself and your needs, which can help you feel more balanced and better able to cope with stress.
- It improves your physical health: Self-care practices, such as exercise, good nutrition, and sleep, can help improve your physical health.
- It enhances your emotional well-being: Taking time to do things you enjoy, connect with others, and express your emotions can all contribute to your emotional well-being.
- It boosts your productivity: When you're well-rested, nourished, and feeling good about yourself, you'll be more productive and able to tackle tasks more effectively.

Chapter 05

Practical Self-Care Strategies

There are many different ways to practice self-care, and what works for one person may not work for another. Here are some ideas for incorporating self-care into your daily routine:

- Take breaks: Make time to step away from your work or other responsibilities and do something you enjoy.
- Exercise: As mentioned in Chapter 3, exercise is a great way to manage stress and improve your physical and emotional well-being.
- Get enough sleep: Good sleep hygiene (as discussed in Chapter 3) is essential for managing stress and improving overall health.
- Eat a healthy diet: Nourish your body with a healthy, balanced diet to help manage stress and improve your overall well-being.
- Make time for activities you enjoy: Whether it's reading, writing, playing an instrument, or something else, make time to do things you enjoy.
- Connect with others: Spend time with loved ones or make an effort to meet new people. Social connections can be a great source of support and can help reduce stress.
- Practice relaxation techniques: Techniques such as deep breathing, meditation, or yoga can help you relax and de-stress.

Chapter 05

Incorporating self-care into your routine takes time and effort, but it's worth it for the benefits it can bring.

In the next chapter, we'll look at how to build resilience, find balance, set boundaries, and seek support from loved ones as you journey toward a stress-less life. Remember, managing anxiety and stress is a lifelong process, but with the right tools and mindset, you can learn to thrive in the modern world.

MOVING FORWARD

As you work to manage your anxiety and stress, it's important to focus on building resilience, finding balance, setting boundaries, and seeking support from loved ones. These strategies can help you navigate life's challenges and maintain a healthy lifestyle.

Building Resilience and Coping Skills

Resilience is the ability to bounce back from adversity or challenges. Building resilience can help you better cope with stress and setbacks, and can help you feel more resilient in the face of future challenges. Some ways to build resilience include:

- Practice gratitude: Focusing on the things you're thankful for can help put challenges in perspective.
- Find a support system: Surround yourself with people who support and encourage you.
- Learn from setbacks: Instead of dwelling on failures or mistakes, try to learn from them and move forward.
- Take care of yourself: As we discussed in Chapter 5, self-care is an important part of building resilience.

Finding Balance and Maintaining a Healthy Lifestyle

Maintaining a healthy lifestyle is key to managing stress and feeling your best. Here are some tips for finding balance and taking care of yourself:

Chapter 06

- Set goals and priorities: Identify what's important to you, and make time for those things.
- Make time for rest and relaxation: It's important to take breaks and recharge.
- Get moving: Exercise and physical activity can help manage stress and improve overall health.
- Eat a healthy diet: As we discussed in Chapter 5, nourishing your body with a healthy, balanced diet is essential for managing stress and improving overall well-being.

Setting Boundaries and Saying No

Setting boundaries and learning to say no can be an important part of managing stress. It's important to know your limits and be honest about what you're able to handle. Here are some tips for setting boundaries and saying no:

- Identify your priorities: Knowing what's important to you can help you set boundaries around your time and energy.
- Communicate your boundaries: Let people know what you're comfortable with and what you're not.
- Practice self-care: Make time for self-care and prioritize your own needs.
- Learn to say no: It's okay to say no to requests or obligations that don't align with your priorities or that exceed your capacity.

Chapter 06

Seeking Support from Loved Ones

As you work to manage stress and anxiety, it's important to seek support from loved ones. Having a supportive network of people you can turn to can make a big difference in your well-being. Here are some ways to seek support from loved ones:

- Talk to someone you trust: Sharing your thoughts and feelings with someone you trust can help you feel less alone and more understood.
- Seek professional help: If you're struggling to cope with stress or anxiety on your own, seeking the help of a mental health professional can be an important step towards improving your well-being.
- Take breaks and spend time with loved ones: Surrounding yourself with supportive people can help you feel more balanced and less overwhelmed.
- Don't be afraid to ask for help: If you're struggling to cope with stress, don't be afraid to reach out to loved ones and ask for help.

In conclusion, managing stress and anxiety is a lifelong process, but with the right tools and mindset, it's possible to live a healthy and fulfilling life. Remember to identify your stress triggers, practice self-care, build resilience, find balance, set boundaries, and seek support from loved ones. With a little effort and dedication, you can overcome anxiety and stress and thrive in the modern world.

CONCLUSION

In conclusion, stress and anxiety can be overwhelming and disruptive, but with the right tools and mindset, it's possible to manage these challenges and live a healthy, fulfilling life.

In this book, we've explored practical strategies for overcoming anxiety and stress, including identifying stress triggers, practicing self-care, building resilience, finding balance, setting boundaries, and seeking support from loved ones.

By implementing these strategies and techniques, you can learn to cope with stress and find peace of mind in the modern world. Remember, managing stress and anxiety is a lifelong process, but with a little effort and dedication, you can overcome these challenges and thrive.

ABOUT THE AUTHOR

Umar Plummer is a writer/musician with a passion for helping others overcome stress and anxiety. With 15 years of experience in the field, Umar Plummer has helped countless individuals learn to manage stress and live healthy, fulfilling life.

ACKNOWNLEDGEMENTS

I would like to express my sincere gratitude to all of the
people who have helped me bring this book to fruition.
First and foremost, I want to thank my family and friends
for their unwavering support and encouragement. Your
love and kindness have meant the world to me, and I
couldn't have done this without you.

I also want to thank my colleagues and mentors in the field
of writing and music, who have taught me so much and
inspired me to pursue my passion for helping others. Your
guidance and expertise have been invaluable.

Finally, I want to thank all of the readers who have taken
the time to read this book. I hope that it has been helpful
and that you are able to use the strategies and techniques
outlined here to manage stress and live a healthy, fulfilling
life.

REFERENCES

1. "The Stress Solution: A Scientific Approach to Managing Stress and Anxiety" by L. J. Davis and J. G. Davis
2. "The Anxiety and Phobia Workbook" by Edmund J. Bourne
3. "The Mindfulness-Based Stress Reduction Workbook" by Bob Stahl and Elisha Goldstein
4. "The Science of Resilience: How to Succeed in Life, Work, and School" by Paul L. Nussbaum and Wendy A. Suzuki
5. "Boundaries: When to Say Yes, How to Say No To Take Control of Your Life" by Henry Cloud and John Townsend
6. "The Healing Power of Supportive Relationships" by Robert A. Neimeyer and Janet L. Sonne
7. "The Science of Well-Being" by Sonja Lyubomirsky
8. "The Happiness Trap: How to Stop Struggling and Start Living" by Russ Harris
9. "The Upside of Stress: Why Stress Is Good for You, and How to Get Good at It" by Kelly McGonigal
10. "The Anxiety Workbook for Teens: Activities to Help You Deal with Anxiety and Worry" by Lisa M. Schab

INDEX

www.ingramcontent.com/pod-product-compliance
Lightning Source LLC
Chambersburg PA
CBHW071217260726
48653CB00041B/1005